HOME OFFICE
PRODUCTIVITY

UNLOCK YOUR ENERGY, PERFORM AT
YOUR BEST EVERY DAY, AND HAVE
MORE TIME TO ENJOY LIFE

BY **KATIE STONE**

Contents

CHAPTER 1

Introduction

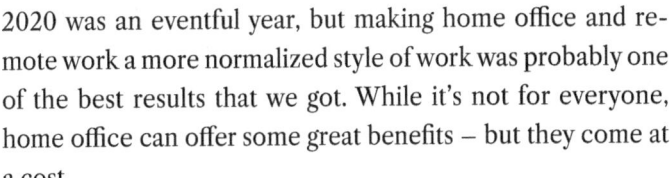

2020 was an eventful year, but making home office and remote work a more normalized style of work was probably one of the best results that we got. While it's not for everyone, home office can offer some great benefits – but they come at a cost.

Keeping the comfort of your own home while also saving time by not having to commute sounds great, until you notice the subtle side effects that slowly creep up on you.

In this book, I hope to help you create a healthy work-life balance at home, focusing not only on increasing your total output but improving the *effectiveness* of your work at home while also keeping you sane.

I believe productivity is not about maximizing your results, but about making sure you are *effective* while you work, so you can have a great and balanced life while you are *not* working.

As always, this book is supposed to be a guideline, not a rule book. Everyone struggles with different problems, has a different job, and a different situation at home. Take away from each chapter what you can, then adapt and modify it to make it best for *you*.

Don't take this as a definitive guide, providing the ultimate truth. Take it as inspiration. Actively read it and implement the ideas you get while reading. I also summarized practical tips and tasks at the end of each sub-chapter—use these as a baseline. But again, don't be afraid to change it so it fits *your* situation!

I hope you will be able to find at least one or two nuggets of wisdom here that will make a big difference to you. It's often the little things – a harmless idea that, once made into a habit, change your life completely.

Look for *those ideas*, the small changes, the simple habits that, over time, have the power to change everything for you.

Good luck!

- Katie

CHAPTER 2
Why You Aren't Productive

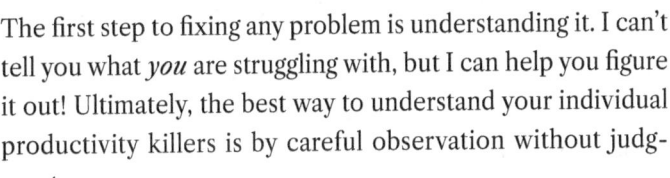

The first step to fixing any problem is understanding it. I can't tell you what *you* are struggling with, but I can help you figure it out! Ultimately, the best way to understand your individual productivity killers is by careful observation without judgment.

Maybe it's your general mood and energy. You get out of bed and already feel like going back. You eventually struggle to your desk with a coffee, but you just can't find the motivation to get anything done.

Maybe you *are* motivated...if there weren't so many things on your plate and constant distractions keeping you from getting any work done.

Or maybe you are simply overloaded and feel like a mountain of work and chores is crushing you, and no matter what you do, it isn't getting smaller!

Whatever it is, you will find a way to first understand your problem and what's really behind it, and then tackle it in small steps. You will notice the first improvements days after starting this process, so keep reading and stick to it!

I have to make a note about expectations, though. You might wish to wake up full of energy, get ten hours of work done before lunch, breeze through the day, and have plenty of energy left in the evening to spend with your family or friends. The truth is, while you might get that on *some* days, it's an unreasonable expectation.

Mental energy is limited; misusing it will wreck you.

Just like photos on Instagram never show reality, listening to "highly productive people" never shows the full picture. A business leader and mentor recently taught me his productivity system, and I was shocked to see that he only has a total of 10-12 hours per *week* of focused work.

It's easy to "never run out of energy" and "always be focused and relaxed" when you work only 10-12 hours per week, rather than 10-12 hours per *day*.

This is not meant as an attack in any way or dismissing his style of work – quite the opposite.

Trying to work 10+ hours a day while staying in peak state is simply not realistic.

It's possible to run a marathon, but you cannot run a marathon *every day*. Recovery is critical, for mental work as much as for physical work.

Another common misconception that I see is that most people want it to be *easy*. And I get that. But the reality is that often, it just won't be. You have to be okay with that – which in turn, will solve the problem you *thought* you had.

Some people, for example, often wake up feeling refreshed, energized, and ready to tackle the day. If you are not one of those people, that doesn't mean that there *has* to be a problem – you might just have a different chronotype.

Personally, I tend to have slow-ish mornings, but I still have plenty of motivation when I'm supposed to go to bed. Once I started working *with* my natural tendencies, I not only became more productive, but also much less troubled by everything I felt was "wrong with me."

If your goal is to "have it all," be warned: your main problem could be the goal itself. Unrealistic expectations hurt us more so than the situation itself. Just like unrealistic expectations for your body can seriously harm your psyche, or unrealistic expectations of the perfect love story can stand in the way of actually finding love.

Think of it like a relationship. Or children. Or pets. Or a hobby. Or almost everything else: It's going to have ups and downs. It's going to require work sometimes. You won't have perfect days every day. So don't be too hard on yourself when some days don't go well. Instead, treat yourself with compassion, especially during these difficult times. Sit down alone for a few minutes and reflect on what went badly that day and how you can try to prevent it in the future.

I'll cover that in more detail in a later chapter, but for now, I wanted to remind you that striving for perfectly productive days, seven days a week, is going to put you under more stress and pressure than the actual work. You don't have to be perfect. You don't have to be able to "do it all" like that coworker supposedly does. They probably struggle just as much as you do; it's just not as obvious.

Especially since you really can't have it all. Yes, maybe that colleague always gets more done despite having a husband and two kids. Maybe she puts in ten-hour days, seemingly with ease, while you struggle to meet your deadlines.

But maybe that's because you still spend time with your husband and make breakfast with your kids every morning while your colleague's marriage is going down the drain.

Try not to compare yourself with others—only with yourself. And always keep in mind that there are two sides to every coin. Sometimes, you might sacrifice productivity for health, your kids, your partner, your pet, or any number of reasons.

That's why I try to focus this book on achieving a *balance*. **My goal is to maximize your productivity while maintaining a healthy balance of your own life, happiness, and health.** If you feel like some tactics or suggestions in this book would mean a significant decrease in quality-of-life for you, don't feel pressured to do it! They are, after all, suggestions. Pick what helps you most, and ignore what isn't helpful in your situation.

And with that, let's move forward to common productivity killers. Some of them may be more applicable to you than others. I will cover each of them more in the following chapters. For now, try to focus only on understanding what keeps you from being your most productive self!

Lack of Energy

On some days, no matter what I do, I feel like I could close my eyes for a second and fall right back asleep. These days suck. It's a constant uphill battle, and while I can get *some* work done with discipline, it's never a lot.

Is coffee a solution? Yes and no. It's a crutch like a band-aid over a bleeding wound. Unless you stop the bleeding, it's not going to get better.

An entire chapter is focused on improving your daily energy. Of course, the foundation is actually getting enough sleep. If you don't get a solid 7-8 hours of quality sleep every night, start there. But there are many reasons why more sleep alone will not fix the problem, which we'll all cover later.

Lack of Motivation

Motivation is a tough nut to crack. When you have it, everything is easy, and you breeze through hours of work. When you don't have it, it feels like every step is a struggle.

Can you fix it? Absolutely! But you'll have to reframe your thinking and may need some proper reasons for work. The Mindset chapter covers that. Because while motivation might *seem* like a fleeting state that you are only sometimes blessed with, it is actually much more under your control than you think. With the right tools, you can boost your motivation to a much higher baseline, so you have it more often and perform better even when you don't.

Lack of Focus

This one's very common yet hard to spot. You may be working ten hours a day but still don't get much done. Without good focus, everything becomes harder than necessary, and the important things don't get crossed off your list as fast. More importantly, depending on your work: You are productive, but do the wrong things – or the right things the wrong way – and in the end, produce low-quality work that doesn't move the needle.

Good news: This problem is covered throughout the entire book! In every chapter, with many actionable tips you implement, you will improve your focus.

Work Overload

In an ideal world, you take on only a reasonable amount of work per week, leaving some extra room for unexpected tasks. You would finish all your work every week and achieve all your goals. But that's likely not the reality for you.

When you are assigned more work than is realistic to finish, you will have to expect a certain amount of overwhelm. While some pressure can be good to push you, too much can erode your focus and drain your energy.

You may not be able to control the work assigned to you, but you can learn to manage your time, focus, and mindset to better deal with overwhelming amounts of work and unrealistic deadlines without losing your sanity, health, or balance.

Distractions

The biggest change from the office to working at home is the number of distractions that constantly surround you. There is wisdom in having a dedicated office, as it can keep you focused.

At home, there are more distractions than most people even realize: It's not just the more interesting activities that tempt you (napping on the couch, Netflix, or playing with your pets), but also the chores that still need doing, tasks that you have put off, and possibly other people who need you for non-work stuff.

From a personal perspective, this can be good – who wouldn't rather spend time with their partner than be in yet another mind-numbing meeting that could have been an email?

However, from a productivity perspective, having so many more interesting options around you constantly can severely impact your focus, while constant reminders of waiting chores can also wreck your energy. Our brains are best suited for one-thing-at-a-time kind of work, and all those little things that are nagging at you cost you more energy than you know.

All this is covered in a section to help you manage this unique challenge as best as possible.

Lack of Tools

Finally, a very situational problem. If you're a programmer used to working on a workstation with three big screens and your colleagues close by for coding help, suddenly working from home on your company laptop will be a huge step backward. Similarly, as a graphic designer, you might be used to big tablets for drawing and powerful computers for rendering 3D models. Or maybe it's as simple as lacking the space for all the reports you used to lay out in front of you daily, not having your favorite pens, or missing your sun-bathed office with enough room to breathe and think.

The best I can offer here—since this is going to be different for everyone—is to either find ways to get what you need or find ways to work with it. That might seem obvious, but simply shifting your focus from complaining to trying to make the best of it can already make a huge impact.

Yes, maybe the computer rendering now takes fifteen minutes instead of two. What a perfect time to check and answer emails or do the dishes! Remember, it is what you make of it. If you only feel bad about it, it will be bad. Try to see the upsides, and it won't make you as miserable.

For example, I had a daily conference call, during which I wasn't really needed and rarely had anything useful for me. At first, I was super annoyed. It cost me time and focus for nothing. Eventually, I started doing stretches and yoga during these fifteen to thirty minutes while on the call. It was a great break, and I could combine a necessity with something *I* cared about!

This is one of those aspects that will likely hurt your productivity, but can actually be useful for more balance – as taking breaks is not only important for recovery, but also for more focused work afterward.

CHAPTER 3

Mindset for Home Office

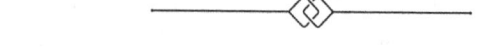

One of my biggest wishes for the future of education is that mindset be given more attention. It's completely ignored almost everywhere, and most people are oblivious to its importance.

Yet it is crucial in every aspect of our lives, every single day. It's the difference between a healthy relationship and constant drama, between a high-achiever and a "loser," between a happy life and daily depression.

Science agrees: "mindset" is in the mind, but it affects your body physically, too. This stuff is real! They even successfully proved that our thoughts and emotions alter our DNA over time. There are also studies that show that merely *imagining* a workout or practice session can have a real impact on physical strength, muscle building, and skill improvement.

But what does this have to do with productivity while working at home?

Everything.

It is the foundation for everything I want to teach you in this book. If your mindset is out of place, it will be hard to control your work life, your balance, and even your happiness.

And since I value that balance and happiness very highly, let's start with that!

The Art of Balance

At home, the lines between work and life blur. In the office, you are usually available while you're there. If you leave the office every day at 5, no one expects you to take a client's call at 6.

But at home, it's different. You're basically in the office 24/7. You could pick up the phone, open the laptop, and log in to the system anytime. If an important email comes in, you *could* respond to it immediately—even if it's 10 pm. That's just going to score bonus points with your boss or the client, right?

The problem is that it usually doesn't. As soon as you start compromising your work-life balance, it will become expected. "But you always respond to emails all day." Will it make you seem more reliable, possibly a better candidate for a promotion? Maybe.

Is it worth it? I say no.

Because if you don't have a time where you truly log off from work, work doesn't end until you sleep. There's always a part of you that's ready, waiting for an email, a call, or worrying about work stuff.

And that takes a heavy toll on you.

We *need* to rest and recover. We sleep not only to recover physically, but mentally as well. Our brains get filled with thoughts, plans, worries, and even fears throughout the day. If you don't "clean up" at night, those feelings will linger and seep into the next day. Soon, they will feel permanent, a constant pressure. But we weren't built for constant mental stress throughout the day—we can't recover from that in a single night.

If you don't want to blow up, you need *daily* recovery time. That includes not only sleeping time, but also free time *without* pressure. You need to be able to switch off. Log out.

I would highly recommend not having work emails on your personal phone if you have a company device. Ideally, when you quit work for the day, make it a point to be unreachable except for emergencies.

That can be a tough line to draw, especially when you feel you "owe" it to your boss or company. But unless you're getting paid to be reachable all day—you don't owe them anything.

Do your best while you're on the clock, be accommodating when you can, but make it clear that your personal time is *your personal time*. When you *do* make an exception, it will also mean a lot more than when you constantly make "exceptions" and let it become normal.

Action steps

Separate your time: Define the time that is "work time," and also add non-negotiable "off-time" to your schedule. The exact time might be company policy, or maybe you have some leeway. For example, if you define an hour as a dedicated lunch break, take that time truly off. Don't even think about work. If someone asks or wants a call/chat/meeting during that time, don't be afraid to decline and say that that's your lunch break. If your company allows you to set your own times, this is your right! (Again, you can make exceptions, but be clear that it is one, or it will become expected over time)

Separate your thoughts: Unless you're on the clock, you don't get paid to worry about future (or past) work-related problems. If you *do* worry, either sit down and actively think about the problem and try to find a solution (and clock in!) or put the worry on a post-it note for tomorrow. Then let it go until you're back at work.

This is not a once-and-done solution but a mindset you likely need to practice for weeks or months. If you need, put it on your to-do list to stick to it. You can also put up post-it notes to remind you of it. Whatever you need to do to successfully stick to it!

Designing your Office Space

To create a healthier work-life balance, it helps to draw a clear line – not only with your time but also with your space. In an ideal world, you have your own "office room," designed and equipped with work in mind—a quiet, peaceful, clean environment where you can focus on work.

Practically, most of us won't have this. But we can do our best to re-create the experience. Here are a few action steps to create a good working space in your home:

Dedicate it for work only. It doesn't matter if it's a desk, a chair, a place in your garden, or a coffee shop. It's a workplace now. You don't relax there. And you don't work somewhere else (most of the time). That helps put you in work mode while you're there and keep you in "life mode" when you're not there.

Keep it tidy. Our brains are built to keep track of our environment constantly to keep us safe. If you have your to-do list on your desk, every time you see it (even in your peripheral vision), your mind will be reminded of all the things you still have to do. *Instant stress!*

Also, is that report lying there unfinished? *More stress!* And the phone? Did I get a new email? Did someone post on Instagram? *Need to check!*

Even if it's not a *conscious* thought, don't be fooled. Your brain is always keeping track of all the things around us. It's what kept us alive when there were still predators hunting us in ancient times.

That same brain has evolved to some extent but fundamentally functions the same. Anything around you is scanned and interpreted constantly. And so, anything that reminds you of something you have to do will put that task – and the guilt of not having done it yet – into your mind. Many of these unfinished tasks pile up quickly and lead to constant overwhelm. That's why a vacation can be so relaxing – there isn't a massive pile of open tasks around you constantly.

The more you declutter, clean up, and structure your home workplace (and home!), the more mental capacity you'll have available.

Make it nice. Why does a spa need peaceful music, beautiful landscapes, fluffy towels, and wonderful scents? Because we relax with all of our senses. We also fear with all of our senses. We love with all of our senses. We *live* through our senses.

So, if you want to feel happier while "at work," make your workplace more than just functional – make it nice. Add a pretty plant or flowers, a photo of loved ones, a subtle decoration, or some scents. If you feel good at your workplace, it will be much easier to spend time in it! Don't overdo it, but put in some time to upgrade your home workplace – it's a great investment.

Creating a place for work at home will help you be "at work" when you work and "go home" when you log off, clock out, or finish for the day. This will make it easier to focus on work and be productive while you're at it and help you relax and enjoy time off when you're done working.

Just because work-life balance is mostly a mindset thing doesn't mean we can't help the mindset with physical tricks! While our thoughts and emotions impact our physical well-being, the physical world also impacts our thoughts and emotions. Even small things, like that thin layer of dust on your screen or the basket of unfinished laundry—reminders of work not yet done—add to your stress.

The fewer things on your mind, the more you can focus on the tasks. Everything that your brain needs to keep track of costs mental energy. Make sure to find ways to "keep your head clear" by only focusing on what's important *now*. By separating your work life and private life, even at home, you basically cut the amount of pressure on yourself in half instead of worrying about everything all the time!

In the Schedules & Routines chapter, we will work on reducing that pressure even further. But first, let's begin with your mornings...

Chapter 4

Morning Routines for Home Office

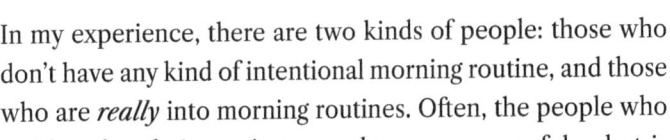

In my experience, there are two kinds of people: those who don't have any kind of intentional morning routine, and those who are *really* into morning routines. Often, the people who highly value their routines are also very successful – but is there a connection?

For me, there are two levels to this: If your job is to make decisions that make or lose millions of dollars or decisions that impact millions of people, you owe it to yourself and the world to be at your absolute best. For this, devoting an entire hour every morning to "sharpening the axe" becomes more than reasonable.

However, for us "normal people," **a morning routine is more like a brief preparation to get us not only ready for the day but also grounded and anchored to our best selves.**

It's not just about "getting more done," but also about how you feel all day, how you show up to the world, to others, to your partner, and to yourself.

However, before we start looking into your daily morning activities, we have to take one step back: Your nighttime activities. What you do before going to bed is as important as what you do after getting up. Studies confirm that your thoughts and mental inputs before bed linger and get processed while you sleep – and so, how you wake up and feel in the morning is a direct reflection of how you went to bed the night before.

By the way, if you want to learn more about morning routines and optimize your well-being, productivity, and energy levels, check out my bestselling book "Morning Rituals" on Amazon!

Great Mornings Start at Night

As I said, a productive morning starts the night before. You might have to make some changes to achieve that.

First, create a routine. Don't go to bed whenever you feel like it—pick a time and stick to it. Start your evening routine about 30 minutes earlier. Consistency is actually quite important, maybe the most important part of an effective evening routine. This sets your circadian rhythm, which is connected to a multitude of health benefits – including deeper sleep and higher energy levels.

If you aim to get eight hours of sleep per night, I recommend setting two timers: one for the start of your routine and one for your actual bedtime. Play around with the length of your routine and sleep time – after all, it needs to fit *you* and your lifestyle.

A healthy evening routine typically includes:

No digital devices. Especially phones are a no-go. Not only do digital screens give off blue light, which disrupts your day-night cycle and makes it harder to fall asleep, but consuming content and information at this time will fill your mind with new (often negative) input rather than allowing it to unwind and process.

Dim the lights. As much as possible, avoid bright lights – sunset-like lighting is optimal: Dim, warm light puts your body in a sleepy mood and promotes peace and relaxation. Candles also work, if you do not have the right lamps for that.

No more work. This may seem obvious, but it's deeper than just "not working" – it also means no more *thinking* about work. The day is over, done, finished. Anything that comes up: Write it down for tomorrow. No more problem-solving today!

Healthy inputs. Specifically, *mental* inputs. Reading a good book, podcasts, or audiobooks are all good options. Careful, though: The mood of your inputs determines your mood in the morning. Something peaceful, relaxing, or inspiring works best. Now is also a good time for affirmations!

Soft physical activity. Stretching, yoga, and other self-care activities also put you in a good state for recovery and relaxation. Apart from the physical benefits, this allows you to shut down better overnight, giving you a fresher start in the morning.

Meditation. Any type of meditation works great – just let your mind drift, shut off the "monkey mind" for a while, and enter a deep state of relaxation. Carrying this state into bed will help you recover better and wake up feeling mentally sharp and focused.

Journaling. A great way to clear your head besides meditation is journaling – writing down any and all thoughts about the day, free-form or with guided prompts. This can not only help you reflect and learn from each day, but also let go of any negative emotions you had about the day.

Start the Day Great

After hours of (hopefully relaxing) sleep, you wake up to a blaring alarm. *Oh god, not again.*

If you hate that, here are three alternate approaches: Sunrise alarm clocks, softer melodies, or rising volume.

Sunrise alarms are great for the colder months when you often get up before the sun. They start out very dim and slowly emit more and more sun-like light. This helps your body to feel like it's now time to wake instead of suddenly being jerked out of sleep in what feels like the middle of the night. Your eyes are actually aware of the lighting in the room, even while you sleep. This is how our bodies know when to wake up naturally – with the rising sun (in theory). Faking a sunrise is thus a great way to slowly ease into wakefulness, rather than being jerked awake while it's still dark.

Using a soft melody, anything from forest sounds to classical music, can also make mornings more peaceful. It's much more pleasant to wake up to the drip-drop of rain and singing birds! Not only consciously, but your subconscious is likely conditioned to associate typical alarm sounds with negative emotions, while soft music, birds, or nature sounds are generally considered "safety sounds" from your nervous system. Hearing birds sing has been shown to calm your nervous system, as our brains are still wired to take that as a sign of a safe environment, as it used to be thousands of years ago.

I also like an alarm that slowly increases in volume. This allows me to wake up to either very quiet, gentle sounds when I'm in light sleep, or for the alarm to get loud until I get pulled out of deep sleep.

Once you hear the alarm, though, there's only one rule: You must get up. No excuses.

This is not only your first "productive" act of the day and reinforces disciplined behavior, but it also conditions you quite fast. Soon, the alarm will trigger an instinct to get up and get stuff done, rather than making you want to snooze and stay in bed.

One more note: If you're not a morning person, you might long for this surreal experience of waking up refreshed and energized. You may have to accept that this won't happen for you. It doesn't have to!

It's actually very natural to wake up sleepy. Remember, just minutes ago, your body was in a coma-like state, physically paralyzed and mentally shut down. It takes about 60 to 90 minutes until your body is fully "recovered" from sleeping. So don't feel bad if you're not at your best five minutes after waking – that's normal!

All right, now you're awake – what's next?

Your Personal Morning Rituals

Your morning routine should be very personalized to your needs, lifestyle, and goals in your day-to-day life. However, there are a few rules you should keep in mind:

Your morning sets the tone. Imagine someone waking up at 5 am and going for a run first thing. That can't be a lazy person, right? Everything you do in the morning tells *yourself* who you are going to be today. If you start by snoozing, you'll be mentally on snooze all day. If you start by being disciplined, consistent, and productive – then this is what your whole day will look like.

That's why I highly recommend not taking on too much – it's better to be consistent with a short and simple routine than try a massive routine and fall short every morning.

Be mindful of all input. Just like at night, your inputs in the morning are extremely powerful. If you start by checking messages or emails, you leave this entirely up to chance. Your first mental input may be stress, drama, pressure, and work problems. That's why I highly recommend leaving your phone OFF overnight – at least turning off all internet connections. Not only that, but leave it off until you finish your morning routine! This way, you have full control over what you let into your mind in this state.

Anchor yourself & create ease. If your "morning self" determines your state of mind for the day, make sure that you use that time to align yourself with the person you *want* to be!

Do at least some of the things your best self would do – this can be a healthy breakfast, a morning run, some educational reading, a brief yoga session, a tough workout, or working on your passion project.

If you follow these guidelines, you will be able to make not only your mornings more productive but your entire day more effective. You can also tap into your best self every day, keep your stress levels down, and feel refreshed and ready every day.

Starting with Focus

The last step of a successful morning is the transition into work. And the worst thing you can do is to just... start. One of the most overwhelming experiences for our brains is a situation where you have a lot of options, need to consider all possible consequences and work on multiple things at the same time.

That's essentially a normal workday for most office workers. Lots of different tasks pile up, interruptions are coming in regularly, and there are always multiple projects that need your attention – often urgently.

The opposite of that would be a single task that you can focus on fully, with no distractions.

While this is unrealistic for most people to keep up all day, you might be able to at least spend the first 30 minutes to two hours at work in this mode. You'll notice that not only can you get a lot more done this way, but it is much less draining than the alternative. You might even find this way of working energizing!

To maintain this mode as much as possible, try implementing these three principles:

Plan ahead: Try to work as much as possible from a list of tasks rather than by gut feeling. If you have a clearly defined list of work that needs doing, you can focus on the doing rather than the "thinking about what needs to be done" – which is incredibly draining. This means:

1) Create a plan for the week – either on Monday or the Friday before. Leave enough time for tasks that come up, but list the big tasks that you want to have completed by the end of the week.

2) Create a task list for every day, but do this the day before. This way, in the morning, you can *directly* start implementing rather than spending precious energy and focus on planning.

Minimize thinking: While this may seem strange in a world that values intellect so highly, it's more often smart to think *less*. Imagine a blank document – you need to create an end-of-year report for your boss. Without any further instructions, there are a million decisions to make. Everything from the color and font choices to the KPIs to include, data sources, visualizations, and so on.

Now imagine, instead, you had an exact template, and all you needed to do was follow 37 exact steps to put the right data into the right fields, and you'd be done. This would not only cost you *far* less time but also far less energy.

As much as possible, break down any bigger tasks or projects into smaller tasks and steps. Especially in the morning, it's best to focus your time on either *making important decisions and strategic planning*, or on work that is *easy* – which just means that you don't have to do a lot of thinking. This way, you can either do your thinking in peak conditions or you can start the day by getting a ton of work done fast.

Avoid interruptions: Just like athletes need to get into a "flow state" to perform at their best, so do you. But even if you don't – each interruption resets you back to zero. It's like a racing car that is slowed to a full stop every time an email comes in... it's never going to win any races.

You're that car, and whenever possible, create blocks for fully focused work. I've learned that it helps to split up your time into time blocks for this. Some time blocks are "interruption-free work," where you do the heavy (mental) lifting and get stuff done, while other time blocks are for responding to emails, chats, meetings, and any other "small stuff."

Depending on your work and role, you will have to find a way to make this work for you, but unless you're very high up in the corporate food chain, you won't be able to fully control this. That's fine. But within the boundaries of what is possible (which is often far more than you might think), try to optimize the way you work around these principles.

Not only to become more effective but also to conserve your energy, focus, and sanity!

Because energy is limited, and if you run out of it every day by lunch, it will not only impact your work but also likely cause you to miss out on life!

So, let's look at a few more ways to both *create* more energy and *preserve* as much as possible.

CHAPTER 5

Getting More Done Effortlessly

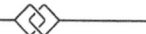

A lack of energy is the most common factor in not only low productivity, but low achievement in general. You might *want* to exercise more, be more social, work on passion projects, and cook healthy meals – but if you don't have any energy, it might stay wishful thoughts forever.

What's important to know is that often, feeling a lack of energy actually has *nothing* to do with energy at all. You might be like a car, fueled up but stuck in first gear. This chapter is all about helping you switch gears and rekindle that fire inside.

That means you will have to employ multiple strategies to "get more energy." Fundamentally, a healthy "normal" is actually *full of energy*, so rather than finding ways to "get more energy," you have to find the problems that *drain* your energy.

Additionally, having energy is not just a state you stumble into, but one that has to be earned. Your brain and body are built to conserve energy, so you have to both train the skill of being *intense* as well as learn to work with your natural wiring to unlock these states.

Finally, after a period of intense exertion, you need to create time to recover. After all, we naturally recharge to full energy, but only if bad habits don't get in the way. Let's start with recovery.

Sleep Quality

For the average person, eight hours of daily sleep is recommended. However, that is only the *quantity*. As you may know, sleep is needed not only for your *physical* relaxation and recovery but also for your *mental* recovery. Dreams are believed to be your subconscious "cleaning up". Even if you think you don't dream—you do. You might not remember them, but you don't need to. Even in non-dream sleep, parts of your brain and nervous system recover.

If you ever doubt the importance of this: There was a study on mice in which the test subjects were prevented from entering REM sleep – the dream state. Those mice died after a few days. And while we are not mice, this still illustrates just how important mental recovery is.

So, how can we boost our sleep quality in terms of mental recovery?

A big part of this recovery is *processing input* – working through all the data your mind has gathered today, making sense of it, fitting it into existing patterns, and storing it for long-term use.

That implies a simple way to improve recovery: Reduce the amount of input. The more information you consume, the more you have to process.

This is not only "information" as in *learning skills*, but absolutely everything. Even just going outside results in a ton of information being absorbed. In recent years, the amount of input has increased massively with the rise of short-form video, which bombards your senses with difficult-to-process information at a rapid pace.

On the positive side, even simple activities like eating, sitting on the toilet, or driving a well-known route can give your mind some time off to process. However, as technology keeps promoting a "monkey mind" mentality, requiring constant entertainment to avoid being alone with your thoughts for even just a few minutes, this happens less and less for most people.

This habit is the most impactful before sleep – the closer to falling asleep, the more dangerous. It's like absorbing information straight into your subconscious, regardless of its content. And let's be real – most of the content in most newsfeeds is either harmless-but-stupid or negative.

Not only will these beliefs, thoughts, and attitudes be absorbed into your subconscious more easily, but they will also be given priority processing because of the recency. You probably have your own experience with this: You're emotionally charged with something as you go to bed, then wake up from a weird dream related to it.

Additionally, as mentioned, we tend to carry our "late-night mood" into the morning. Go to bed stressed out about the economy, wake up stressed out and anxious.

So, my advice is simple: Reduce the amount of useless information and content you consume – especially negative or disempowering input – and completely avoid any *unintentional* input at night. A good book, podcast, or audiobook can be okay, but I try to keep that at least 30 minutes before bedtime, no later.

Action Steps

When you go to bed, make it a habit to leave the worries and stress of the day behind. You can sit down for a few minutes and meditate before going to sleep. Focus on letting all thoughts about the day go. Whenever a thought pops up, redirect your attention to your breathing, for example. It's hard at first, but the calmness that follows is worth it! This can significantly help you mentally relax at night, fall asleep faster, and wake up more refreshed.

Even better, start leaving your day behind not when you go to bed but a little earlier, as described in the Morning Routines chapter. Don't see sleep as something you have to go through. Treasure it. Respect your sleep. To make this easier, start minimizing the use of electronic devices and information consumption at least an hour before bed. Start going inward and going slow, rather than being constantly outward-focused, consuming, and busy at a fast pace at all times. It takes practice at first, but the payoff is worth it.

Lack of Focus

Alright, you followed your new evening routine, recovered well, and went through your morning routine. You're off to a great start and feel good about yourself. And yet, at the end of the day, you realize that you haven't really accomplished anything. Why does that happen?

You've probably heard about being "in the zone"—the mystical place where top athletes go to break world records and win championships. Well, you can go there, too!

When you see athletes on TV—runners, football players, tennis players, or even chess champions... do you ever see them on their phones? Talking to a teammate about the weekend they had?

No, they are 101% focused on the game. They have trained the skill to get into and stay in the zone.

Sadly, this is not a skill set that is even remotely taught in schools, universities, or workplaces. So, if you want to be a high performer or high achiever, it's a skill you need to teach yourself. Let's start with the foundation: Focus.

As with everything, I am a big advocate of understanding your primal nature and working *with* it, rather than trying to force yourself against it.

Look at our eyes, for example. Generally, animals have developed to help them survive or thrive. For "prey animals," eyes are on the side for best all-around awareness. But for predators, eyes are at the front so they can fully focus on their target and take it down.

But we are also, like most animals, *motion-focused.* That's why "staying still" is an almost universal instinct to stay hidden, and why most animals look around to make sure they are safe – to detect movement of possible threats.

It's important to understand that survival is always prioritized – if you're trying to focus on a target but detect a threat moving in, that threat is now your focus.

In modern times, a "threat" is often very different from threats in the past. This can be seeing your boss walk in your direction, a new email that pops up, or an annoying co-worker entering the room.

The good news is that many of these distractions are eliminated when you're working from home – big win. However, you might have just as many – if not more – distractions at home. And all of these will wreck your productivity and drain your energy if you don't intentionally manage them.

Basically, we are hard-wired to react to distractions, even when we focus on a target.

Every email that pops up, every notification, every unexpected call, even that dog that barks outside—they all pull our attention away from the task you are trying to focus on.

But even worse—*switching* focus costs mental energy. Working on a single thing for an hour is much less exhausting than working on six tasks for ten minutes each—*especially* if you make progress on each, but don't finish any of them.

Often, a distraction becomes a "mini-task." You get a message, so you briefly respond. It may only take a minute, but it can cost you ten minutes of focused work. And if there's an emotional charge attached to it – for example, if you are reminded of a deadline – this one message can easily cost you an hour of effective work time.

Every time you switch from writing a report to responding to an email to checking your calendar to calling a colleague to pull data from the system, your brain has to reorganize and pull out the information you need right now. That costs energy!

Some are "mindless" tasks—those are usually not much of a problem. Doing laundry, dishes, brushing your teeth. You don't need to think about these.

But as soon as brainpower is involved, you should do your best to stay on *one* task as long as you can, then take a brief break for just a minute before moving on to the next. (And "break" means *step away*, not check your emails! That's already a new task!)

Your brain is possibly your most important organ and tool for productivity and success. Treat it as well as you can! Just because it doesn't hurt or scream when you overwork it (not until it's too late), doesn't mean it can take everything you put it through.

Action steps

To use your time and energy effectively, you need to focus on focused work. That means:

Working on the right tasks. As covered before, you should have a clear list of tasks that you should be working on right now to get the most done, to make the most progress, or get the best results with your time.

Working in time blocks. As much as possible, especially for important mind-heavy work, block out some time and focus fully on those without switching tasks at all.

Mute interruptions. As much as possible, while in a focused time block, disable all notifications. This can mean closing your email software, setting your mode to *do not disturb* on messaging apps, and putting your phone on silent. If you don't live alone, a sign on your door (if you have one) to prevent others from barging in can also help. While you may not be able to do this as much as you might like in your job, you might find that even just small distraction-free time blocks make a massive difference.

Minimize distractions. Your environment around your workplace in your home should be as distraction-free as possible. Take the time to clean it up, either before work or at night. An unfinished task constantly in the back of your mind costs a lot more mental energy than just *getting it done now*. If you notice getting distracted by something, take note and adjust your space as necessary.

Creating Routines. One of my favorite practices for focus is to include any task that has to be done regularly in a fixed routine or pre-plan it. This way, you don't have to think about it. For example, I like planning my meals in advance or even meal-prepping for the week. This takes a massive load off my mind since I don't have to think about anything at lunchtime. The more you can minimize unimportant thinking and planning, the more mental capacity you have for important work.

When you follow all of these practices, you will soon notice a steep increase in energy and productivity. Focused work seems to drain your energy much less, so you not only get more done but also feel better afterward. It's a win-win.

I also find that knowing in advance *what* to work on makes it much easier to start and keep going. Especially when it's so easy to give in to distractions at home, making work feel effortless is a huge step towards staying on task!

Now the question is... why *should* you develop so much focus when it would be so much easier to scroll on your phone, watch Netflix while working, or play with your dog instead of listening in a meeting?

Finding Purpose

One of the reasons why humans have developed to be the dominant species on our planet is that we are *lazy*, but have the ability to think ahead. This means we are able to do work *now* for a positive outcome *in the future*, but we only want to do that if it makes life easier for us.

For example, instead of going hunting every day, our ancestors started developing traps that essentially do the work for us. They developed tools that make work easier and found ways to get more out of less.

There are many ways to do as little work as possible without getting fired, but I don't want to focus on that; quite the opposite.

Whenever you feel unmotivated to get work done, you'll likely find that it is work that you simply don't care about. You don't feel like you get anything out of it. In a situation like this, it's only natural not to do it – it sounds like a waste of energy, anyway.

If you want to break out of this rut, you need to find reasons to work that you care about personally. This could be career progression, a promotion, or a bonus – but also the emotional satisfaction of being the best in your department, getting great feedback from clients, or proving your haters wrong.

First, "getting things done" is an important part of any motivational strategy. If you feel like work is never-ending, it will wreck you. Instead, have daily, weekly, and even monthly goals that you can work toward and achieve. If you don't regularly feel like you have completed your work for the day, week, or month, you're missing out on a lot of motivation.

Next, you need to go within yourself and figure out what actually matters to you. You might find that the job you're in won't provide that. It's no shame to admit that and start looking at something that would excite you more!

But if you *can* find meaning in your current job or company, make that your focus. It doesn't need to be some grand goal or make the world a better place. It can be as trivial as getting better KPIs than the annoying colleague, getting a promotion that no one thought you could get, or being the best at what you do.

Just remember that you're not going to be able to fool around here – it's your own brain you have to convince, and it will know when you're trying to fake it. Once you *do* find something that excites you, though, you probably will never need another book about productivity again.

Chapter 6
Schedules & Routines

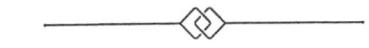

You have probably heard Steve Jobs, among many others, wore the same outfit every single day. While that is quite extreme, as is to be expected of eccentric billionaires, it points out a very important fact: **Every decision costs energy, and making sure you make as few meaningless decisions as possible is a cornerstone of productivity.**

A great comparison is your phone. Remember the old "dumb" phones that could do nothing but call and write texts? Well, they had a battery that lasted a week or more. Now, modern smartphones with far more advanced batteries still run out within a day. Why? *Because we use our phones that much.* Everything you do costs power. Every email that is downloaded, every time you refresh your feed. Keeping track of where you are and waiting for messages constantly drains the battery.

Decisions are exactly the same. Only in real life, you don't have a display that shows your current energy level. But what you *can* do is to be very self-aware and observant.

Try to remember a very relaxed vacation day. You wake up, enjoy the sun shining through the windows, maybe go downstairs to the hotel dining hall for the breakfast buffet, then walk along the beach and swim in the ocean. Life is good.

Or, on a regular workday, where you already have things to worry about before you even had breakfast, and a hundred different things need your attention as soon as you log in. You have to make *decisions*. Not all are conscious. But all of them take energy.

On the beach, you barely have any decisions to make, and most of them don't matter. There are no consequences. It doesn't matter if you bring one or the other towel. It *does* matter if you send that report with your boss in CC or not. That might have consequences. Our brains are trained to think ahead, simulate what the involved people might do or say, and keep a dozen factors in mind to *predict the future*.

That's one of the crucial advantages we humans have over other species. Predicting outcomes based on our experience is an incredible skill. But it's intense work, even if we barely notice.

You take a ten-minute work break. You could do laundry. Do the dishes. Tidy up the living room. Or sit on the couch and stare into nothingness. *And is it too early for a glass of wine?*

For each of these choices, you'd subconsciously think ahead. *If you do the laundry now, you don't have to do it later. But the washing machine might get loud right when you have a call. Maybe the dishes, instead. But that might take a little longer than ten minutes. I could tidy up, then, but that might take even longer. I shouldn't just do nothing, though!*

Different sides of you fight for making the decision: the side that wants to get things done versus the side that is lazy, the perfectionist side versus the side that just wants to get it over with. Different factors influence the decision.

To minimize this massive energy drain, we need to find a better way to manage our work.

Creating a Routine

How much do you think when you take a shower in the morning? (or evening) Not at all, probably. You wash yourself in the same order every day, then dry yourself the same way, and eventually brush your teeth in the same way as always. That's your brain already optimizing decisions away.

We can do the same for our workdays and make decisions in advance. But not only that, we can decide *once* how we want to do things, and then just follow our routine day in, day out.

For example: *Every day at 10 am and 2 pm, I take a fifteen-minute break. If there's laundry to do, I do that. If not, I do the dishes. If both are already done, I take a walk around the house. Also, every Wednesday and Saturday at 9 am, I water the plants.*

A routine like that eliminates many small decisions in your daily life, which will make you feel significantly less exhausted by the time you reach the afternoon. They also help stay on track—it's much easier to remember to water the plants if you do it at the same time on the same day(s) every week!

Ideally, you can get to the point where by the time you log into work, you have made no more than maybe three decisions at most. Develop your own morning routine and follow it every day. If you live alone, this will be easy. If you live with your partner, roommates, or even with kids, this will, of course, be more difficult. But that's okay! You don't have to be like a robot without the capacity to adapt.

So, how do you get started with this approach?

Think about all the small chores and tasks that come up regularly and create a list. Throughout the day, be mindful of tasks you forgot and add them to the list. For as many as possible (or reasonable), find a fixed time to do them.

Another option is to group a few of those together and create a time block in your calendar. For example, a half-hour block for "household chores." Whenever new household work comes up, you can put it on a separate to-do list and then work through this list during the allocated time block.

The important part is this: When you schedule work for later, or add it to a routine, you essentially banish it from your mind. You intentionally remove it from your mind by putting it on a list with a clear time and date. This way, you don't remember it or keep it in mind.

This is the important part – you actually have to let the task go and stop thinking about it. If you feel like something is unresolved, resolve it until you can let it go and move on. This may take some practice at first, but being able to actively remove things from your mind is a massive step towards feeling light and unburdened all day.

If you're worried about this mindset making your life too rigid, don't worry – adapt it however you see fit. It's supposed to be a toolbox for implementing basic principles that *support you*. If you find certain methods are too restrictive, don't use them!

For me, a little routine is comfortable. I like following the same steps every morning. I like cleaning my home every Sunday, so I never have to worry about it.

But I couldn't possibly eat the same foods every day at the same time. Not only do I enjoy variety too much, but I also want to stay flexible with my schedule so I can eat when I actually *want to*, not when I "should" eat.

Figure out what works best for you, and don't be afraid to adapt your routines and schedules again and again. As long as you and your life change, so will your routines.

CHAPTER 7

Journaling

———◇———

It's a strategy not exclusive to being more effective working from home, but in my opinion, one of the best things you can do for almost anything. There are hundreds of ways to journal, from personal diaries to bullet journals to written to-do lists and more.

I do a simple combination of daily reflection and gratitude, which I highly recommend in times of chaos and change. Reflection helps you adapt faster and thrive, while gratitude helps you become more resilient, appreciative, and fulfilled. Let's start with reflecting.

Reflection

Every morning, write down the most important goals for the day – almost never more than three. If you can check them off in the evening, you should feel satisfied for the day. That's the basic premise of both a to-do list and productivity in general – not only getting things done, but feeling good about it.

This is not limited to work goals, either, but can include personal goals or tasks as well! For example, you could summarize work as "keep all three meetings today productive" and add "go to the park with the kids" and "clean the kitchen." If you do all three, you do well at work, take some time for your family, and get chores done. A successful day!

The point of this daily exercise is precisely that. First, it creates focus on what's important. You are less likely to procrastinate by writing your goals down, since you *want* to check it off in the evening. Writing it down is you saying to yourself, "Hey, this matters, I want to do this."

That not only keeps you from procrastinating but also from losing focus – you don't just want to "get work done"; you want to get *this* work done!

Then, in the evening, when you do the evening journaling session, you can check these tasks off. Because, as humans, it's easy to focus on the negative parts. On everything we *didn't* do. Coming back to your original goals reminds you of what you *did* accomplish.

Often, we feel like we haven't done enough. Like we were supposed to do a hundred more things today. Being able to say that you have achieved the goals you set in the morning will help you keep those feelings away and bring you satisfaction and a sense of accomplishment instead.

What I then like to add is a simple pair of questions:

- What did I do well today?

- What have I learned for the future?

With this, you can write down what you are proud of today. That can be anything from "delivered a great presentation" to "didn't slap my coworker for being so damn annoying." Writing these things down reminds you of everything you did well, so you don't dwell too much on the bad things that happened. Because usually, we do better than we think once we dig a little deeper!

And the second part is just as important: What have I learned for the future?

You might notice that the question isn't "What did I do badly?" as that helps no one. Instead, it focuses on the positive—how can you improve? What can you do differently tomorrow? It's just a different frame for "what could I have done better today," but from a perspective of "this is what I WILL do better in the future."

Writing down just one or two things every day quickly helps you internalize changes and make them a habit. It can also help you break out of a cycle of "do badly – regret – repeat" by not focusing on what happened, but on what you want to happen *next time*.

Imagine it like driving a car. If you accidentally scratch a parked car and then turn your head as you drive to look back, you're probably going to hit something again. Instead, focusing on making improvements for the future allows you to keep looking forward and drive more safely.

The next day, when you encounter the same situation again—you'll remember. Writing down something is proven to improve recall. Doing it every time you run into the same situation will soon tip the scales, and you'll find yourself doing the right thing and leaving behind negative habits!

This way, you can get a little better every day and prevent endless cycles of negative behavior. It also helps you with a little structure and focus on the positive in stressful and chaotic times!

Action steps

Get a journal or notebook and start taking just a minute every morning and evening for just three simple questions:

- Morning:

  ○ What will I achieve today?

- Evening:

  ○ What did I do well today?

  ○ What have I learned for the future?

Write down one to three goals, and try to find at least one or two things for the evening questions. You can be honest and genuine here – no need to impress anyone. This is only for you, so don't be afraid to admit to things that could have gone better! (But also, don't be afraid to write down how awesome you've been today!)

Gratitude

There are plenty of studies that show the positive effects of gratitude. In short, it helps you with relationships with other people—colleagues, friends, and romantic relationships. It also improves your happiness and well-being while also reducing stress and frustrations. It even helps your self-esteem and improves your sleep!

If you want to learn more, there are hundreds of great articles and books on the topic. I won't cover all the details here, but I want to show you how easy it can be to include it in your daily journaling routine and how it can help you specifically.

The most basic question I would suggest is simply: "What am I grateful for today?"

Write this down after your two evening questions, and try to find at least one or two things *every single day* that made you happy. Yes, even on a bad day, even when everything went wrong.

Not only will this help you put yourself in a better mood before bed, but it will also anchor you to positivity and keep negative thoughts under control. Also, when you feel like the week has been going horribly—you can go back through previous entries and read through all the good things that happened.

This can be as simple as "I enjoyed five minutes in the sun today" or something bigger like "amazing night out with friends." It can be a compliment you got or a lucky coincidence that was on your side. Anything that made you smile and made your day a little brighter.

A significant aspect of happiness is how you perceive things. Gratitude helps you see the best of every day, not only while you write it down, but throughout the entire day. It can be a constant light that brightens up your days and changes negative situations into positive ones simply by looking at them differently. After all, it's not what happens to us, but *how we perceive* what happens, that decides whether we are happy or sad!

Action steps

In addition to the reflection questions, write down the things that made you smile with a question like 'What am I grateful for today?'

This will keep you grounded and improve your mental fortitude and stability by anchoring you to positive thinking and all the *good* things, even in bad times. This gives you the strength to push through hard times, even when nothing seems to go your way.

CHAPTER 8

Recovery & Relaxation

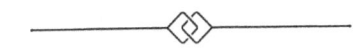

By now, you should see that being effective at work is about more than just the work itself – a lot of the factors are in what you do *outside* of work. In this case, it's about how well you can recover between work sessions. This topic is not exclusive to working from home, but it's even more important when there is no clear boundary between work time and personal life.

Because of this, I have split up this chapter into two separate parts, like two sides of the same coin: How to prioritize and use off-time for recovery to improve your own quality of life, and on the other side, how to recover for more productivity and output during work hours.

Boosting Quality of Life

Some of the biggest obstacles between us and having a blissful evening are often work-related stress, pressure, guilt over leaving work unfinished, and worrying about work problems even when you're not working.

During home office, more than ever, work life bleeds into personal life just as much as the other way around. However, there is usually significantly more pressure and negative energy in your work life, which you certainly don't want to invade your personal life.

One crucial element of having a healthy work-life balance is being able to separate the two. For many self-employed people and business owners, work and life often blend together. Integrating the two into a blend can work well, but nonetheless requires firm boundaries. When you spend quality time with your partner, friends, kids, or even in the gym, kitchen, or relaxing outside – you want to be 100% present and enjoy this time, rather than being dragged down by work-related thoughts.

Often, a "lack of balance" is not about the *time* you spend on each side, but toxic work problems invading your private time. Short term, this will impact your happiness and recovery, as you are burdened 24/7. Long term, this can not only lead to a chronic lack of joy and fulfillment in life, but to serious physical symptoms, as well. Stress often shows up as digestive issues, acne breakouts, and constant restlessness.

So, how do we fix this?

Separating work time and personal time as much as possible is foundational to this. Your subconscious is constantly working to find solutions – as long as you feed it problems. Ideally, you could have total "work amnesia" when you log off until you log in again. Since that is not an option, do your best to keep your mind away from work as much as you can. To make this easier, try to be as unreachable as you can when you're off the clock. Simply knowing that there *could* be an important email coming at any time will make a part of your mind in "work mode" constantly.

Export all thinking when you log off. What I mean is: before you end your work day, write down any "open thoughts" in a work notebook (physical or digital) for tomorrow. If there's a problem you haven't solved yet, write it down as a task for tomorrow. Write down *everything* that's important – to give your mind permission to "let go" of all these thoughts, decisions, and mental notes. This helps clear your mind, signaling your brain to *stop* dwelling on these topics until tomorrow. You literally schedule worrying for tomorrow during work hours to "un-schedule" it for today.

Have a shut-down ritual. Just like an evening routine before bed, have a short little routine before you log off work. Check off your work to-do list, write down tasks for tomorrow, check your calendar, and make any notes that you might need for tomorrow. Have a ritual that clearly signals the end of the workday. Think of the work like an ex – if you don't officially end it, they might linger around, trying to get back with you.

Have a restart ritual. After ending the workday properly, I found it helps to take a few minutes before going back to your personal life. Meditate for a few minutes, or simply take a 10-minute power nap. Let your brain clean up a bit before refocusing on personal plans for the day.

With all these systems in place, you should be off to a great start in terms of separating work and life. In theory, this means you now have a few hours to yourself to enjoy any way you want. But what if that's not the case?

The sad reality for many professionals is that after a full day of work, growing responsibilities, encroaching deadlines, and constant problem-solving, there is not much energy left to enjoy the few hours that remain.

Which makes a lot of sense when you compare the life we evolved to live with the life we are currently living. Our minds have to deal with 100x more input now compared to just a few hundred years ago – which, in terms of evolution, is just a blink of an eye.

The same applies to mental output. While it's true that our ancestors had it "more difficult," going hunting for food or going hungry to bed, the opposite is true as well. During a hunt, much time would be spent in "idle," walking and searching, but with minimal effort. Like any predator, we evolved for short bursts of intensity, balanced out by long stretches of low-effort work and times of complete rest.

All that means that your problem is not that you are "already" tired after eight hours of work, but that you were never meant to spend that much time in intense work every day!

To counter this, learn from our ancestors: you need time off. This means specifically *not* more input – no TV, phone, or any other form of entertainment. Take a walk by yourself, enjoying the sun, chirping birds, and fresh breeze on your face. Go for some exercise, no matter if it's running, weight training, or a yoga session. Stop using your brain for a while and enjoy simple activities, or even doing nothing at all.

Think of your perfect vacation. Whether it's a day at the beach or exploring a foreign city, it's likely a simple activity that you enjoy. "Enjoy" is the key here – it's a verb, the process of actively enjoying a certain situation or activity.

If you don't intentionally take time to actively enjoy simple, "slow" activities during your time off, it might feel like a constant blur of work, entertainment, sleep, work, and repeat.

Slowing down and being more present is the antidote.

Boosting Productivity

If you would rather get more done, maybe because you are building a future for yourself, similar rules apply. If you disrespect your physical and mental recovery, you will pay the price. Not only twenty years down the road but in your daily work.

Being able to recover fully between work sessions also means starting every day at 100% rather than half-empty and sluggish. Once again, my word choice is very intentional: Recover, not relax.

The difference between recovery and relaxation is mostly the intensity, especially for your brain. Think of it this way: When you're sprinting, walking for a while is a *relaxed* pace – but you're still walking. But when you're done, to *recover*, you need the right food, maybe some electrolytes, and plenty of restful sleep.

The same applies to your brain: If you've been thinking and problem-solving all day, anything that's thinking or problem-solving is not recovery. More mental input is also not recovery – this applies to books and audiobooks as much as to watching TV, Netflix, or scrolling social media feeds.

When you start using this perspective during your free time, you might notice that almost all your daily activities are *relaxing* at best, but not recovery. No wonder you are always out of energy, then, right?

It's absolutely fine to spend time either "only" relaxing, or even fully active. Intense workouts, for example, are a good balance if you're mostly mentally stimulated during work. Going out with friends can also be very beneficial, even though it's not always relaxing.

However – if you are *constantly* active, either consuming input or producing output, you need to take a *real* break every once in a while.

Examples include a relaxed walk outside, meditation, or a slow yoga session. Painting, journaling, or mindful cooking can also work. You'll know you're in recovery mode when you feel your mind emptying and quieting down, a sense of calmness and peace spreading.

While some of these might *feel* unproductive (they technically are), you might end up getting a lot more done when you take the time to truly recover, rather than just slowing down for a moment.

Especially when you are trying to solve a complex problem, time off is often the best way to solve it. Switch up your environment, your inputs, or your thought patterns. Because your subconscious is constantly working with all available inputs and past experiences to solve problems, introducing new foreign input can be a great way to solve problems creatively.

Walks in nature, a visit to a zoo, or a dance class can be great places for inspiration. Reading books about all kinds of topics can give you a more multi-dimensional understanding in your specific field, and surrounding yourself with new people for a while can give you entirely new perspectives.

Productivity is not just about how much you work; it's about how effective you are when you work and what you work *with*.

Being productive with your time off means deep recovery and creating depth to your life and experience that will set you apart from everyone else.

CHAPTER 9

Next Steps

———◇———

You are now equipped with many new tools and ideas, but that alone won't make a difference unless you *implement them!*

Don't expect immediate results for everything – it often takes a few days to settle into a new routine and feel comfortable. To form a new habit, you will even have to stick to it for 30 to 60 days.

But as I said in the introduction, It's the small changes that add up over time. A little more energy here, a little less stress there, and soon, you will feel like a whole new person. Whatever routines and habits you start doing, you will also get better at them over time, making them even more effective.

You don't get massive results from *starting,* but from *sticking to the habits* for months. Don't get discouraged – be patient. Big payoffs don't come to people who give up easily.

It's a little bit like working out. You don't see massive results after the second session. It's a habit you stick to, a lifestyle with significant, long-term results and benefits as long as you keep going.

Start small. Start with a single change. After a week, once you get used to it, expand that change or add a second. Make your life better one little step at a time. In a year from now, you'll be *miles* ahead.

Life is not what happens to us; it's what we make of it.

If you believe in yourself and believe in improving your life every day, you will find happiness and success. And it all starts with implementing small improvements daily.

Who of your friends (or colleagues) deserves more success and achievement?

Share this book with them so they can implement these strategies and see the same results as you. Or, even better, do it together as accountability buddies! This will help you both stick to it more easily and have more fun on this journey.

And, if you're interested in getting even *better* results, also get a copy of my book Morning Rituals to be at your best all day, every day with just a few minutes each morning.

Can't wait to hear what you think of it!

Chapter 10

Give and Receive

I firmly believe that if you do good deeds and show kindness to the world, you will receive the same in return – often in unexpected ways, but always more than you gave.

These books are my contribution to making the world a better place, and there is a simple way for you to make an impact as well:

Please leave a short review and share your biggest learnings and breakthroughs with others so more readers will find this book.

The more people read these books, the more people I can help – and the bigger our impact on the world... together.

It only takes a few seconds, but these small acts of kindness and contribution will make not only the world but also your life a better place.

Taking only ten seconds to write a review could...

...help someone get their degree and dream career
...help someone raise healthier kids by being able to spend

more time with them

...help someone improve their well-being and health by finally following healthy habits

...help someone create something amazing that will change the world

Many of the greatest inventors, businesspeople, and creators had defining moments in their path that set them up for success – often, it was a small act of kindness from someone else who had no idea how massive the impact of their small deed would be.

So please, take a few seconds and **<u>leave a Review</u>** for this book.

You can also scan this QR Code to be taken straight to the review page:

Thank you for making a difference – for me, for future readers, and for the world.

Love,
Katie